AF249029

Overcoming Materialism

Gordon G. Talbot

HERALD PRESS
Scottdale, Pennsylvania
Kitchener, Ontario

OVERCOMING MATERIALISM
Copyright © 1977 by Herald Press, Scottdale Pa. 15683
    Published simultaneously in Canada by Herald Press,
    Kitchener, Ont. N2G 4M5
Library of Congress Catalog Card Number: 76-47341
International Standard Book Number: 0-8361-1810-3
Printed in the United States of America
Design: Alice B. Shetler

Contents

Author's Preface

Those of us living in the fourth quarter of the twentieth century have much for which to be thankful. Science and technology have given us many marvelous things to enjoy. However, along with these has come a certain "leanness of soul" growing out of the fact that "a man's life does not consist in the abundance of his possessions" (Luke 12:15).

Recessions, unemployment, and inflation have forced us all to stop and contemplate where we are going. Hopefully, out of this assessment will come a return to appreciation of spiritual values which have somehow been shunted aside in recent years. It is my desire that this book will help readers get pointed in the right direction.

Gordon G. Talbot, PhD
Glen Cove, Maine

1   Examining the Problem

"Take heed, and beware of all covetousness; for a man's life does not consist in the abundance of his possessions" *(Luke 12:15).*

Materialism may be seen as a philosophical theory which explains the universe strictly in terms of the existence and nature of matter. It may be seen as an ethical principle that material well-being should govern an individual's behavior. It may be seen as a personal tendency to give material things undue importance in one's life.

No matter how materialism is viewed, it becomes a problem to anyone claiming to be a child of God. The Christian knows there is more to this universe than natural phenomena. He knows he must be governed by more than material self-interest. He knows that concern for what is spiritual and eternal must take precedence over what is physical and temporal.

Historically speaking, recruits for Christianity have come more from the common masses than from the limited elite. The impact of democracy in recent generations has produced a middle class which now predominates in the societies of many countries. In spite of high taxation, inflation, and other economic obstacles, individuals may still move upward from poverty to moderate affluence. Christians moving upward in the economic scale find themselves subjected to increasing pressures from materialism.

Momentum of affluence

The momentum of affluence begins long before a person acquires much of this world's goods. Within him is the natural desire not only to survive but also to enjoy all the good things he can get for himself. Little children are typically acquisitive, taking whatever attracts their interest, unless it is denied them in some way. Their rooms become cluttered with items they consider valuable and must be cleaned up periodically because of parental insistence. As they develop through childhood and adolescence, their cravings increase.

We have all heard the saying that "the more you have, the more you want." By the time most people reach adulthood, their attitude regarding materialism is fairly well set. Those who acquired many things along the way have a desire for more things than those who have not been blessed with much. The momentum of affluence has begun its work in their lives.

Affluence is, of course, a relative thing. Americans make up about 6 percent of the world's population, but they use up over half of its material goods and about a third of its energy sources. The average middle-class American's lifestyle is opulent when compared with that of many individuals in underdeveloped nations.

Recent changes in economics are going to bring about some drastic upheavals in living styles in the years ahead. West Germany, which enjoyed an amazing economic boom following defeat in World War II, has had

8

the largest monetary surplus among the world's nations, but it is expected that Saudi Arabia will soon pass it in this respect, due to the quadrupled price of oil on world markets. Floating on a "sea of oil" buried beneath its drifting sands, this Middle Eastern country has a problem of trying to decide what to do with its fabulous wealth.

Materialism is something which can affect anyone, whether he is rich or poor. Those who have little can develop a craving which masters them, influencing all they think, say, or do. A poor person may let materialism consume him all his life. Whether he ever succeeds in getting all he wants is beside the point. The momentum of affuence is stronger with those who are able to acquire some of the things they want and who see means by which they can get more.

Covetousness as idolatry

In Colossians 3:5, the Apostle Paul referred to "covetousness, which is idolatry." In other words, Paul defined idolatry as anything which captures the allegiance of a person. The ancient Jews repeatedly turned to literal idols prior to the Babylonian captivity in 587 B.C. Following that traumatic experience, they gave up literal idolatry, but they were often guilty of figurative idolatry. The same has been true of Gentiles as they moved from primitive to sophisticated cultural levels. Figurative idolatry is just as real as literal idolatry, but it is more subtle and harder to detect.

In telling the parable of the rich fool, Jesus spoke of a man who had a bountiful crop of grain on his farm one year (Luke 12:16-21). God had given him that crop, but the man evidently felt no gratitude to Him. He was a selfish man. Instead of sharing his bounty with the poor of his area, he decided to tear down his granaries and build bigger ones in which to store the surplus. Then he planned to sit back and take it easy, enjoying the good life ahead for several years.

It was a jolting experience for him to be visited by God and told that his soul would be required of him that very night. He would have to leave his wealth behind for others. Refusing to lay up treasure in heaven by helping God's needy creatures, that farmer died an impoverished man, for he was not rich toward God.

It may seem strange that Jesus used that parable in warning people against covetousness (Luke 12:15). After all, the farmer had not coveted what someone else had nor tried to take it from him. Actually, Jesus was simply making the point that "a man's life does not consist in the abundance of his possessions."

Let's take it a step further, for we know that coveting describes a craving for what belongs to others. The tenth commandment says, "You shall not covet your neighbor's house; you shall not covet your neighbor's wife, or his manservant, or his maidservant, or his ox, or his ass, or anything that is your neighbor's" (Exodus 20:17).

Coveting is an internal sin, and others do not know it is there unless it is shown in some way. However, coveting has led many people to break other commandments having to do with such things as murder, adultery, stealing, and bearing false witness against others (Exodus 20:13-16).

There are two main ways to acquire money or material things. The first is to have it given to you by inheritance, payment for goods or services rendered, or

10

as a gift. The second is to take it from someone else, either by fraud or outright robbery. Coveting naturally leads to the second type if it is allowed to become overpowering enough to prompt open action.

It seems obvious that covetousness and spiritual growth are mutually exclusive. Where one operates, the other withers. The cure for covetousness, then, would appear to be a determination to draw closer to the Lord through the various ministries available from the Holy Spirit. By giving ourselves to God, we give ourselves to other people as well, rather than trying to take from them what they have.

Displacement of devotion

Materialism leads to covetousness, and covetousness leads to idolatry. Devotion to money and the things it can buy produces a displacement of devotion which belongs to God alone. If there is one thing which God desires from us above all other things, it is our loyalty and devotion. Anything which threatens to impinge on that causes Him grief. It can also cause sorrow to the person involved.

This was the problem facing the rich young ruler who came to Jesus to ask what he might do to inherit eternal life (Matthew 19:16-22). When Jesus instructed him to sell all he had, give the proceeds to the poor, and follow Him, the young man "went away sorrowful; for he had great possessions." They meant more to him than devotion to Christ did.

Jesus then remarked to His disciples that it was very difficult for a rich man to enter the kingdom of heaven (Matthew 19:23-26). They were amazed at this, for they held the common notion that a rich man must be close to God, or God would not bless him with material wealth. When they asked who then could be saved, Jesus simply replied, "With God all things are possible." He might have referred them to Psalm 37:35, 36, which shows that God sometimes allows even evil men to prosper temporarily before cutting them off without warning.

Peter then took it upon himself to ask Jesus what reward the disciples would get for their devotion to Him (Matthew 19:27-29). Jesus said that they would reign with Him in His kingdom (cf. 2 Timothy 2:12). He also said that everyone who had given up all to follow Him would be rewarded a hundredfold and inherit everlasting life.

Devotion directed toward oneself lies underneath devotion to money or what money can buy. God created us to bring praise to Himself, not to ourselves. Therefore, He will not honor selfishness. The fruits of selfish behavior may bring comforts and pleasures in this life, but they bear within themselves the seeds of judgment.

Devotion directed toward the Lord assures a person of eternal blessings, as well as a life of spiritual blessings on this earth. Those who are farsighted enough to realize this can plan their lives accordingly. Grappling with materialism is one way to face up to this responsibility.

2   Considering Status Symbols

"What is your life? For you are a mist that appears for a little time and then vanishes" (James 4:14).

If a man's life does not consist in the abundance of his possessions, then what does give life meaning? Many people see money or material things simply as the means by which they may acquire more intangible possessions. As far as they are concerned, wealth becomes the currency by which they buy such things as prestige, security, and various kinds of power.

Individuals employ a wide range of status symbols to set themselves apart from others and make themselves feel superior. Physical appearance depends a great deal on natural endowments at birth, but billions of dollars are spent each year by people trying to improve their appearance. Mental ability is largely determined at birth, but educational systems employ more people than any other field of human endeavor in an attempt to help students live up to their potential.

Above and beyond physical and mental endowments, people seek to acquire other status symbols which they are convinced will give them an edge over the majority. If their life is but a vapor, puff of smoke, or a mist which will soon vanish, then they want to get the most out of it

13

they can while it lasts. Pursuit of prestige, security, and power is often a disappointing or dangerous business, but this does not deter them from engaging in it.

Money and prestige

There was a time when sheer brute force was enough to push a man to the top position within his tribe. That is still often the case among primitive cultures today. It is also usually true within groups of children at play. However, in more sophisticated groupings brute force is not sufficient to earn instant prestige. More subtle techniques are used.

Everywhere we go there are signs that money produces prestige. An individual's clothing is a factor in prestige. The fashionably dressed person automatically gets more respect paid to him than the shabbily clad person. The make, model, year, and condition of the automobile one drives is important to most people. The neighborhood and kind of residence one lives in gives some idea of financial and social standing. Where one's children attend college makes a difference. Where a person spends his vacation gives him a certain ranking.

There is a sense in which prestige can be purchased, as noted above. However, there is prestige which the expenditure of money alone cannot buy. Brash people with newly acquired wealth may find it extremely difficult to find acceptance with old-line aristocrats because they lack what might be called "proper breeding." Top executive positions in corporations are often reserved for individuals with superior leadership abilities, regardless of the size of their bank accounts. Top government posts are subject to the will of the electorate, and money may become an obstacle to confirma-

14

tion, as happened in the case of Nelson Rockefeller when he was nominated by Gerald Ford for vice-president of the United States.

Nevertheless, money does carry great weight in today's society. Athletes and entertainers burst out of obscurity almost overnight, earn fabulous sums in a short time, and find themselves lionized by others. The same thing can happen to an author, an inventor, or even a social critic. Participants in the Watergate scandal or its cover-up have come out of prison to write books or hit the lecture trail, thus replenishing their bank accounts by telling of their experiences. We might say that even notorious prestige sometimes has its monetary rewards.

God has His own way of evaluating such developments, of course. His sovereign will may be credited with the sudden fall from prestige which some individuals experience. Both money and the prestige it may buy can disappear as a drifting vapor.

Money and security

People who have much money are normally very security-conscious. In a world where crime is on the increase they have every reason to be cautious. There are always plenty of people around them who would like to separate them from their wealth.

Factories, mines, stores, and other places which generate wealth are often shielded from outsiders by elaborate identification and security devices and personnel. The residences of wealthy people sometimes make use of sophisticated surveillance systems to protect them from intruders. The fear of robbery, kidnapping, and extortion calls forth procedures designed to prevent the rich from being victimized.

In spite of the dangers associated with being wealthy, most people would take the risk if the opportunity to be rich offered itself to them. In fact, they think of possession of money as one of the greatest forms of security they could acquire. Fear of poverty and the suffering and embarrassment it can bring is a powerful motivation to accumulate wealth, if possible.

Those who have always had enough funds to pay for the things they have needed and some of the luxuries they have wanted cannot know the terrible feeling which poor people have. As a result, they are often insensitive toward them and fail to take any personal interest in them. Since the government makes itself responsible for welfare programs, private citizens leave themselves out of such situations to a large extent. Some even look down on people who, through no fault of their own, are unable to care for their own needs.

Surely, this is an unchristian attitude and is condemned by the Word of God. King Solomon gave good advice when he said, "He who is kind to the poor lends to the Lord, and he will repay him for his deed" (Proverbs 19:17). Solomon also said, "Cast your bread upon the waters, for you will find it after many days" (Ecclesiastes 11:1).

Security cannot be found in possession of money alone. During the Great Depression some men of wealth who lost everything committed suicide by jumping from skyscrapers in financial centers. Both money and the security it may buy can disappear as a drifting vapor.

Money and power

We live in a power-conscious society, as we suddenly learned in 1974 when the Arab embargo on oil plunged the world into a crisis with extensive consequences. The concern for energy resources ran head on into concern for protection of the ecology, and modifications regarding conservation of the environment had to be made. For example, the stalemated Alaskan pipeline project to bring oil down from the north slope to the seaport of Valdez was quickly reactivated, in spite of threats to the ecology on the tundra and elsewhere.

In the 1960s and 1970s we were bombarded with various kinds of people-power, such as black-power, red-power, and others. Organization of minorities and their demand for equal rights made a significant impact on society and brought about some societal reforms. In some cases, they may have gone too far and then had to suffer the backlash of the majority, but substantial gains were made on the whole.

Political power has been a factor of life within democratic societies for a long time. However, the existence of political machines of the old corrupt nature evidently has passed its heyday. People are better educated now, more aware of current events, and quite conscious of what political maneuvering can do to government systems.

Terrorism has been increasing in recent years all over the world. Assassinations, bombings, and rioting are now reported so frequently that they have become almost commonplace. By such tactics small and shadowy groups keep whole nations in a state of agitation and uneasiness and open the door for totalitarian measures from the far left or the far right. Such power is far out of proportion to the numbers involved or the causes they uphold.

On a personal level, individuals have found that

money often makes it possible to gain power over others. Those in desperate circumstances will often do anything to get money, so those who have money can manipulate them at will. It is possible in some situations to buy a position of leadership and influence in various fields of human activity. A large contribution to a political candidate's campaign fund has been known to have the power to "buy" an ambassadorship in recent years.

Once in power, a person may learn to cash in on his investment. The dictator of a small country is ousted from power, but he lives in luxury while in exile somewhere else. A corporation executive embezzles hundreds of thousands of dollars from his firm and moves to a country with no extradition treaty with his homeland. A crime syndicate boss guns down his opposition and then rakes in the profits from the rackets he controls.

Money may help a person get power, and power may help him get more money, but both can be taken away in a moment. One well-placed bullet, a sudden heart attack, or an ingenious move by an ambitious underling, and all is lost. Both money and the power it may buy can disappear as a wisp of smoke.

3   Desiring the Simple Life

"I would have you wise as to what is good and guileless as to what is evil" (Romans 16:19).

The Amplified Bible translates the latter half of Romans 16:19 as follows: "I would have you well-versed and wise as to what is good, and innocent and guileless as to what is evil." In this we see reflected the philosophy that the simple life, rather than the worldly-wise life, is better. When Jesus saw Nathanael coming to Him early in His ministry, He said, "Behold, an Israelite indeed, in whom is no guile!" (John 1:47). In this way he commended Nathanael for his openness and lack of deceit.

There seems to be a kind of sanctified naiveté which God desires for His children. Instead of being caught up in the usual whirl of attitudes and actions typical of this world-system, they are to live differently. Their interest in status symbols will be different. Their social ambitions will be different. Their set of priorities will be different. It is not that they should be unaware of what is going on in their world, but rather that they will not become enmeshed in its materialistic gears and the evils resulting from them. This may not be easy, but it is important for those who would be faithful.

19

The guileless life

Artificial mannerisms displayed by others are hard for all of us to bear. Their attempts to make us believe they are something they are not tend to disgust us. We have to take an objective look at ourselves to see if we, too, are guilty of affectation. No doubt all of us can discover some of this trait in our lives, and we should determine to eliminate it as soon as possible.

The guileless life is the truthful life. It does not practice deception to make impressions on others which do not reflect what we really are. We may be candid, but not tactless. We may be frank, but not blunt. Diplomacy needs to be practiced along with truthfulness. So-called "white lies" are no more acceptable with God than "black lies" are, but we can learn how to lovingly spare the feelings of others without them.

Humility is needed in the guileless life. Paul said, "For by the grace given to me I bid every one among you not to think of himself more highly than he ought to think, but to think with sober judgment, each according to the measure of faith which God has assigned him" (Romans 12:3). Later in the same chapter, he returned to this thought by saying, "Do not be haughty, but associate with the lowly; never be conceited" (Romans 12:16). It is the man with a haughty spirit who needs to fear a fall (Proverbs 16:18).

Acquisition of status symbols by expenditures of money should be avoided by Christians. This practice tends to foster a spirit of pride within them. They fall into the trap of trying to elicit praise and respect from others for what they *have,* rather than what they *are.* It takes money away from the Lord's work. It puts people on an economic treadmill which enslaves them. It should be accepted as a tactic of Satan, and he ought to be kept "from gaining the advantage over us; for we are not ignorant of his designs" (2 Corinthians 2:11).

Avoid social climbing

We all know what "trying to keep up with the Joneses" means, and we may have been guilty of it ourselves. The basic motivation for this, of course, is pride. We don't want our relatives, friends, neighbors, business associates, or others to appear to be getting ahead of us in any way because that would indicate that they are better than we. Conversely, if we trade down on our next house or automobile, we are afraid others will think we are inferior human beings.

Many young people in recent years expressed their dissatisfaction with the adult establishment by turning their backs on materialism. This was evident in their grooming, dress, activities, and even housing, if they lived apart from their families. However, there has been a swing of the pendulum back toward materialism again. Most college students interviewed regarding life goals express a desire to have all the status symbols of previous generations. The influence of materialism dies hard, probably because it is tied to personal pride.

What is the alternative for Christians? Obviously, it is to live as simply, economically, and unostentatiously as possible. This is the way Jesus and His disciples lived during their ministry on earth. In the thirteenth century, Francis of Assisi and his disciples reverted to this manner of living. In both cases, these men were bucking the lifestyles maintained by religious leaders of their times. Christians today are going to have to do the same, if they want to imitate them.

There are some practical advantages to living the simple life. Many pressures are reduced. Less physical and mental exertion is required to keep up with a reduced budget. The fast pace of life can be slowed down, a point especially important to people as they get older. Many anxieties and frustrations melt away. There is time for other activities previously postponed.

One of the greatest blessings is the freedom to be of greater service to God and to one's fellowmen. There are many deeds of kindness we all know we should do, but we often find no time to do them. By living the simple life, we can get them done. This will help our testimony and perhaps open doors for witnessing which we have not had before.

It is unlikely that "the Joneses" will even notice we have abandoned plans to keep up with them. They may notice it and decide to cut back on their own ambitious plans for social climbing through overspending. If a chain reaction is set up within our own circle of acquaintances, that could benefit all. We just have to make sure we don't let the economists persuade us we are unpatriotic for not boosting the economy. They never did offer to pay the bills we ran up by overextending our credit, anyway!

Ordering our priorities

Materialism does not lend itself well to serious determination of priorities. Much money is spent as the result of impulse buying. We see something that attracts us, we build up a tremendous desire to acquire it, and then we try to squeeze it into an already overloaded budget. Only later do we come to our senses and wish we had been more deliberate about buying the item.

22

Every Christian entering the labor market or inheriting funds should sit down and draw up a list of the things he considers most important in life. Naturally, he should consider God's work first and place that at the top of his list, planning to set aside what belongs to Him. Then there are the normal necessities of life, such as food, clothing, shelter, medical and dental care, insurance, taxes, utilities, transportation, and others.

Any surplus left over can go in several directions. It is a blessing to share some of it with those in the Lord's work or those in need. Paul told the Ephesian elders that they should remember "the words of the Lord Jesus, how he said, 'It is more blessed to give than to receive' " (Acts 20:35). We might use some of the surplus for building up an emergency fund for times when the regular budget is strained beyond the breaking point. We might invest some in stocks or bonds which will provide added income. We ought to do something to prepare for old age and a loss of earned income, supplementing what is available through social security programs.

We have to realize, of course, that certain situations can alter any carefully planned budget with its list of priorities. Debilitating illness or a death in the family may require drastic changes. Loss of a job, involvement in a massive accident, destruction of one's home by fire or hurricane, and other disastrous influences can call for a new ordering of priorities. However, it is good to keep in mind that the three general categories mentioned above should be followed whenever possible—God's work first, normal necessities second, and surplus expenditures third.

Reverting to the simple life can be almost traumatic

because it almost always has to be done in one grand move. It is unlikely that it will come through gradual cutting back, although that is not impossible and may even be preferable. Human nature is such that the quick cutback seems to work better than the gradual cutback. There is kind of an excitement to making up one's mind and then following through on it as soon as possible.

Once the simple life is achieved, the problem of maintaining it must be faced. There will be the usual pressures to get back to the status quo. A gradual erosion of determination to keep life simple will probably threaten the new lifestyle. It might be helpful to write up a covenant stating what you want to do, with God's help, and then keep it with other important papers so it may be taken out and read periodically. Members of the family can check on each other and speak up when they see will power fail.

Desiring the simple life, taking the steps necessary to get it, and then maintaining it can be a deeply spiritual experience. The Lord will honor those who seek to imitate the lifestyle His Son demonstrated while He was on earth, especially if they do it so they may be of more service to Him.

4   Studying Human Experiments

"And all who believed were together and had all things in common" (Acts 2:44).

Plato advocated community of property in the *Republic.* The Essenes practiced a communal form of life two centuries before Christ. The early Christians in Jerusalem had all things common. There is an interest in communal living threading its way through man's history.

In 1516 a book entitled *Utopia,* written by Sir Thomas More, was published. It was a satire, for More was thinking of England when he wrote of the imaginary island of Utopia as an ideal commonwealth. The perfection in law, politics, and other aspects of national life he described were impractical, so the word "utopian" has become synonymous with "visionary" ever since. However, that has not prevented men from attempting to establish utopias.

Some of these experiments have passed away quickly, while others have endured for many years. One of the characteristics of a utopian organization has been isolationism from normal forms of society. In our world we have found that isolationism simply isn't practical. Modern men are too interdependent to go it alone. Even

when self-sufficient primitive tribes are discovered, it is
not long before they begin to share the blessings, and the
curses, of modern life. In our brief study of human experiments in communal living, we must be realistic
enough to take note of the prevailing trends of our
times.

The early church experiment

About three thousand Jews in Jerusalem were
converted to Christ and baptized in His name on the
Day of Pentecost. They quickly formed themselves into
a distinct group of believers known as followers of "the
way" of Jesus the Nazarene. They suspended their
normal occupations and devoted themselves exclusively
to a program of learning, praying, and evangelizing. To
support such a program, they voluntarily sold the
properties they owned and deposited the proceeds in the
common treasury of the church. The money was drawn
upon as needed to supply each one with the necessities
of life. From this developed the slogan used by communes since that time, "From each according to his
ability, to each according to his need."

The early Christians made their rounds each day,
visiting the temple and the homes of anyone willing to
invite them to break bread. The joyous mood of these
believers was attractive and contagious so that they
"were having favor with all the people" in Jerusalem. As
a result, many conversions were made. "And the Lord
added to their number day by day those who were being
saved" (Acts 2:47). It was not long before "the number
of the men came to about five thousand" (Acts 4:4).

The early church commune was evidently broken up
after several months by various persecutions instigated

26

by the leaders of Judaism. The most severe was that led by a fanatical young Pharisee named Saul, who later was himself converted and renamed Paul (Acts 8:1-4; 9:1-22). It is logical to assume that those who survived the persecutions went back to their normal occupations and ways of life. Nowhere in the Scriptures do we find Christians instructed to reestablish the communal pattern, although we are admonished to maintain a strong fellowship as the family of God. The New Testament epistles teach Christians to live righteously within society, drawing apart frequently in local assemblies for mutual experiences of worship, instruction, fellowship, and service opportunities.

Those who argue that Christianity supports the establishment of socialistic or communistic forms of government should take note of certain factors operating in the early church. The motivation for selling goods and giving the money to the apostles was that of love, not government legislation. The timing was important, for the early Christians set up a special way of life for a limited time to get the gospel out as quickly as possible. This short-lived experiment ought not be used as a model for a permanent mode of societal organization. Indeed, experience has shown that most similar experiments have lasted but short times or undergone modifications which allowed them to continue longer.

Various utopian experiments

Various monastic orders in the Middle Ages were communal in nature. The Albigenses sought to introduce communal systems in France and soon failed.

Hutterites deserve special mention here, for they have maintained a communal way of life a long time. Originally Austrian peasants they moved eastward across Europe to the Russian Ukraine before coming to America in the 1870s. Persecuted as conscientious objectors during World War I, many moved to Canada. Today there are about 8,000 in the States and 15,000 in Canada, located on scattered communal farms, or *Brüderhofs*.

Taking Acts 2:44 as their model, Hutterites have "all things in common." Work is done collectively under the leadership of elected lay preachers and bosses, or *Wirts*. They attempt to be self-sufficient, but they do use modern farm machinery and send their children to public schools. Crime, mental disorders, and other social problems are rare in their close-knit communities.

Jesuits set up an Indian republic of thirty communal mission villages in Paraguay from 1609 to 1767. Early English settlements in North America featured common property at first, but this was soon abandoned.

The writings of Sir Thomas More and of French philosophers, such as Jean Jacques Rousseau, encouraged an interest in communal forms of government. Through the influence of Louis Blanc a shift was made to state control, rather than individual cooperative effort, in bringing about social reforms.

In the early nineteenth century, Robert Owens, a Welsh manufacturer, encouraged the formation of cooperative groups of 500 to 1,000 persons, in which land and tools were commonly owned and shared, as well as the harvests which resulted. Several such colonies were started in England and the United States, but they didn't last long.

As North America developed during the eighteenth and nineteenth centuries, an atmosphere for social experimentation was provided by the availability of cheap land and a nonrestrictive government. The Seventh-Day Baptists had a community at Ephrata, Pennsylvania, from 1732 to the end of that century. The Shakers established one at Watervliet, New York, in 1774, later moving to New Harmony and Economy, Indiana, and dissolving in 1906.

A German Separatist sect began a community at Zoar, Ohio, in 1819. The Amana Community, starting near Buffalo, New York, in 1842, moved to Iowa in 1855, filling seven villages. French communists lived in Texas in 1848, moved to Illinois, and finally settled in Icaria, Iowa, to prosper until 1895. Other groups which might be mentioned are the Perfectionists at Oneida, New York (1848), the Fourierians at Brook Farm and other communities (1840s and 1850s), the Ruskin Cooperative Colony (1894-1902), the Christian Commonwealth of Georgia (1896-1900), and the Freedom Colony of Kansas (1897-1905).

Perhaps the best known of these has been the Amana Community of Iowa because of the nationally advertised line of kitchen appliances manufactured there. In 1932 that community of seven villages abandoned some of their communal practices and set up a stock corporation involving 1,300 persons.

Isolationism and interdependence

Although these utopian communities usually grew out of social or religious motivations, there was an economic factor also involved. It was felt that common ownership and sharing of land and implements would benefit everyone in the community. Duplication of expenses could be eliminated. Humility of spirit could be fostered, for individuals would not be tempted to brag about their accumulation of private possessions. In cases where religious beliefs were strong, it was felt that self-contained communities could keep evil influences from penetrating and influencing its members, especially the young.

Isolationism became characteristic of utopian communities. However, it is difficult to sustain continued isolation from the rest of the world. As time went by, the isolationism began to break down. Curiosity about the "outside world" was a powerful motivator to break out of the restrictions imposed on a community's members. Opportunities from outside beckoned. The basic desire for private ownership of property and goods took its toll. Dissatisfaction with prevailing leaders made some want to leave.

We live increasingly in a world where individuals are dependent on others. Pioneering days are pretty much over now. Goods and services flow across nations and across continents to meet worldwide needs. There are few places left on earth where a small group of isolationists can homestead land and put down their roots. The constant flow of new products from today's scientific research and technology are hard to resist. Idealism comes up against the hard fact that life can be much easier, if people will cooperate with one another, not only within a particular community, but between communities, states or provinces, and nations.

If we are going to find the simple life mentioned in Chapter 3, we shall have to search for it in the midst of an interdependent society and world. In other words, we need to resist the evils surrounding us and hold firmly to the good things we want. Our sense of community can center in neighborhoods, churches, and groups important to us. Then, by God's grace, we can try to penetrate society with the Christian message and perhaps persuade others to join us in living as the people of God.

5   Seeking God's Will

"Do not be foolish, but understand what the will of the Lord is" (Ephesians 5:17).

Nothing is more important in this life than to know God's will and to do it. This affects all aspects of our lives, including our attitude toward material things and our use of them. Every time we have to make a decision, whether it is a large or small one, we ought to consider what God would have us do.

Robert Rouse of London, England, may well have wished he had had divine guidance when buying a British Leyland Rover 3500. It was reported that the car was out of operation for 114 days during his first 165 days of ownership. The car cost $7,750, so one would expect it to be sound. However, it required three new engines, two gearboxes, two bell housings, and new wiring during its first 6,000 miles on the road. It received the "Square Wheel Award" from *Drive,* official magazine of the British Automobile Association, for 1975. The award was based on a survey of motorists' complaints. This is not meant to denigrate the automobile company which made it. Every company produces a "lemon" now and then.

The point to be made here is simple that material

things do play a big part in our lives, and we need to know God's will regarding them. The problem is in knowing how to determine His will. This chapter is devoted to suggestions for solving that problem.

Divine resources available

As in all things, we should turn to the Lord for help in solving any problem. If we want to know His will, what resources does He make available to us for knowing it?

First, we can study the Bible to know God's will. The Word of God is an extension of Himself, and that is what makes it as eternal as He Himself is. God's will always lines up with God's Word. There are both positive and negative principles to guide us in the Bible. In some cases, we learn what He wants us to do, and in some cases we learn what He forbids us to do. No amount of rationalization can change these eternal principles. We need to learn them and live by them, or we can be chastised. Because spiritual realities are declared more important than material things, we ought to emphasize them in any decisions we make.

Second, we can commit ourselves completely to the Lord. It should be obvious to us that God more readily reveals His will to those who are yielded to Him than He does to those who are not. When material needs press in on us, we can transfer them to the Lord. Peter wrote, "Humble yourselves therefore under the mighty hand of God, that in due time he may exalt you. Cast all your anxieties on him, for he cares about you" (1 Peter 5:6, 7).

Third, we can pray for guidance from the Lord. Paul wrote, "Have no anxiety about anything, but in everything by prayer and supplication with thanksgiving let your requests be made known to God" (Philippians 4:6).

When praying, we must be sure we leave the results in the Lord's capable hands. He may grant our requests, deny them, or tell us to wait for answers. We can thank Him for whatever His reply may be, for He knows what is best for us, and that includes material things.

Fourth, we can learn to be patient. God works according to His own schedules, not ours. If we try to run ahead of Him, we may cut ourselves off and regret it. David wrote, "Be still before the Lord, and wait patiently for him" (Psalm 37:7). The verb "wait" and the adverb "patiently" comprise one word in the Hebrew. If we are not waiting patiently, then we are not waiting according to God's definition. A decision to buy a house, an automobile, or any other big item has to contend with human impulses and cravings, but these must take second place to the will of God. Waiting for His answer can be frustrating, but it is best in the end.

Fifth, we can know God's peace in our hearts. We can depend on it that we have determined God's will only if peace accompanies it. To claim to know His will but still be in inner turmoil about it is ridiculous. Paul said that those who pray can claim "the peace of God, which passes all understanding" (Philippians 4:7). This applies to spending of money just the same as it does to other things.

Sixth, in the Christian community, the family of God can surround each member, counsel one another, and seek God's will together. As Paul exhorted in Colossians 3:16, "Let the word of Christ dwell in you richly, teach and admonish one another in all wisdom."

Human resources available

Some help comes from heaven, and some help comes

from earth, as far as determining God's will for our lives is concerned.

First, we should use our basic intelligence. Our minds are not like the mind of God, for we are limited in our thoughts. However, He has endowed every normal person with some measure of intelligence and He expects us to use it in making decisions. It is probably safe to say that most of our problems are to be solved through use of whatever intelligence we already have or acquire. We have the ability to compare quality, prices, and other factors when purchasing various items we need.

Second, we should face ourselves in a realistic manner. God's will is more likely to be revealed to us in the areas of our strengths than in the areas of our weaknesses. If we insist on trying to achieve in fields where we obviously do not have natural talents, or in areas which we seem unable to acquire talents, we may find it self-defeating. It seems wiser to seek achievement in fields where we can succeed. It could be that God keeps some of us on modest incomes because He knows that is all we can handle.

Third, we should seek the advice of experts. Solomon wrote, "In an abundance of counselors there is safety" (Proverbs 11:14). Life is too complicated for us to do everything for ourselves today. Hosts of experts in various fields can help us with our problems. We should thank God for them and use their talents to meet our needs. Some people don't really know how to manage their resources. An expert in money management might help them get stabilized, teach them to stop being wasteful, and even help them increase savings or make it possible to contribute more to God's work.

Fourth, we should take advantage of circumstances.
Both God and men open certain doors of opportunity
for us and close others. The Lord always wants what is
best for us, although men may thwart our plans. God
can overrule in difficult circumstances, and He will, if
that is what He wants for us and we are trusting in Him.
However, it seems logical to assume that we ought to
walk through open doors, rather than pounding in frustration on closed doors. This can have many applications in our approach to material things.

Fifth, we should remain flexible. God's will for us is
unchangeable, but it may appear to us sometimes as if it
changes. The point is that we have to be flexible enough
to follow His plan for our lives, no matter how many
strange or unexpected turns it takes. The ability to
adjust to change is a human resource. When we have it,
we can see God's will as something cumulative, rather
than isolated. It grows and develops through the years in
successive layers.   Paul said, "I have learned, in
whatever state I am, to be content. I know how to be
abased [destitute], and I know how to abound; in any
and all circumstances I have learned the secret of facing
plenty and hunger, abundance and want. I can do all
things [God requires of me] in him who strengthens me"
(Philippians 4:11-13).

The decision-making process

A situation develops, and we know it has to be re-
solved. We may put it off for a while, hoping something
will happen to resolve it, but nothing does. When the
pressure gets great enough, we must face the problem
and seek to solve it. A decision must be made. It cannot
be avoided or ignored any longer. The decision-making

36

process begins to operate.

How can we seek to deal with situations and be sure we are doing it within God's will? There can be no one formula for any and all situations, but general principles provide us with a framework within which God can work. The suggestions already given in this chapter can be utilized.

Seek divine resources. Make sure you are guided by biblical principles. Commit yourself completely to the Lord. Pray for His guidance. Wait patiently until He makes His will clear and plain. Don't make a move until His peace fills your heart.

Seek human resources. Use the brain the Lord gave you to its full potential. Face yourself realistically, stressing your strengths, instead of your weaknesses. When necessary, seek the advice of experts. Take advantage of circumstances featuring open doors, and don't pound in frustration on closed doors. Remain flexible, able to change and adjust, realizing God's will for you may point you in new directions you had not expected.

All Christians are stewards of whatever resources God permits them to have. It may be His will for some of us to have very little of this world's goods, while He wants others to have much. We may go through both thick and thin periods over the course of our lives. All that really matters is that we remain pliable in God's hands. Then, whether we have little or much, we can be content.

6   Establishing a Goal

"There is great gain in godliness with contentment" (1 Timothy 6:6).

What does it take to make a person content? The answers to that question could be as varied as individuals are. Surely, one of the reasons people crave material things is that they seek pleasure, power, and attention. Therefore, the desire for material things can be physical or psychological in origin, and sometimes it is difficult to tell which it is.

Cheree Taylor, 7, of Titusville, Florida, ate very little at home. Her parents had to force her to eat. They sought medical advice for their skinny daughter. Then Cheree entered an eating contest at the Fourth of July picnic, and everything changed.

She put down eleven hard-boiled eggs in four minutes, came in second in the pie-eating event, and then finished off with six cotton candies, six ice cream cones, fried chicken, potato salad, and baked beans. The amazing thing is that since that time this 55-pound girl has eaten more than anyone else in the family daily. Cheree claimed she was hungry, but we cannot help but wonder if the attention she received from heavy eating satisfied a psychological craving stronger than a physical one.

38

This chapter seeks to show that there is a spiritual goal which can outweigh both physical and psychological goals. It certainly can be stronger than a material goal. We are talking about the goal of godliness, a genuine source of contentment for those who have experienced it and cultivated its growth in their lives.

Christian maturity analyzed

Many misconceptions regarding the nature of Christian maturity have floated around the evangelical world in the past, and they continue to do so today. People deceive themselves into thinking they are deeply spiritual because they talk much about spiritual things, live by a rigid legalistic code, hold to a particular theological position, or are extremely busy in the Lord's work. Beneath all this, however, they know they are spiritually shallow and desperately in need of new spiritual development.

What is Christian maturity? It is a quality of life in which born-again believers are under the control of the Holy Spirit. In brief, it is Christlikeness. The believer who is truly spiritual gives evidence of the fruit of the Spirit in his life—"love, joy, peace, patience, kindness, goodness, faithfulness, gentleness, self-control" (Galatians 5:22, 23). It all condenses down to right living or godliness.

"Every good endowment and every perfect gift is from above, coming down from the Father of lights" (James 1:17). We know that a sinner is made righteous by placing his faith in Jesus Christ, God's Son, who became a sin-bearer for all men. "For our sake he made him to be sin who knew no sin, so that in him we might become the righteousness of God" (2 Corinthians 5:21). We know that every spiritual advancement a believer makes is under the guidance of the Holy Spirit. That is why Paul urged believers to "be 'filled with the Spirit' " (Ephesians 5:18).

This means that God, through His Son and through His Spirit, makes it possible for us to know spiritual realities. We can share in the divine nature by claiming the promises God has given us (2 Peter 1:4). No greater privilege, nor responsibility, has ever been offered to men than this. It is unfortunate that only a comparative few have availed themselves of it.

True godliness is bound to affect a person's attitude toward material things. Paul wrote, "We brought nothing into this world, and we cannot take anything out of the world; but if we have food and clothing, with these we shall be content. But those who desire to be rich fall into temptation, into a snare, into many senseless and hurtful desires that plunge men into ruin and destruction. For the love of money is the root of all evils; it is through this craving that some have wandered away from the faith and pierced their hearts with many pangs.

"But as for you, man of god, shun all this; aim at righteousness, godliness, faith, love, steadfastness, gentleness" (1 Timothy 6:7-11). That is a powerful statement, indeed!

Ramifications for time

If we accept Paul's desire for godliness as our own goal in life, then we must come face to face with certain ramifications of it. These apply to our lives here on earth. Later in the chapter, we will deal with ramifications of the goal for our lives in heaven.

If godliness is our goal, it will affect our physical lives. We dare not indulge in gluttony, drunkenness, sexual immorality, abuse of others, or any other practices which are ungodly. We must keep our bodies in as good condition as possible, available to God for His service.

If godliness is our goal, it will affect our mental activities. We dare not indulge in skepticism, sinful rationalizations, erotic thinking, or any other practices which are ungodly. We must keep our minds constantly renewed by saturating them with the principles of God's Word. We must be under the perpetual tutelage of the Holy Spirit.

If godliness is our goal, it will affect our emotional behavior. We dare not indulge in losing our temper, giving way to depression, hating others, or any other practices which are ungodly. We must keep ourselves tenderhearted, trusting in God, and forgiving.

If godliness is our goal, it will affect our social contacts. We dare not indulge in personality clashes, snobbishness, ostracism, or any other practices which are ungodly. We must keep ourselves loving, humble, and concerned about the feelings of others.

If godliness is our goal, it will affect our material outlook. We dare not indulge in coveting, stealing, dispossession tactics, or any other practices which are ungodly. We must keep ourselves generous, sacrificial, and informed about the needs of others.

No area of our lives is outside the influence of our basic goal of godliness, righteousness, or holiness, including that of our material concerns. If we fall down in this one area, we will find it affects the other areas, too. Truly spiritual people do not divorce their material interests from the rest of their concerns.

We have been told we should live every day with eternity's values in view. That is good theology. A Christian is not completely earthbound. He can lift up his eyes to the future that awaits him in heaven. That gives him a proper perspective and the motivation to keep living for God until Christ comes back to take him to his eternal home.

If you study 1 Timothy 6:1-6, from which our key verse for the chapter came, you will note that Paul dealt with a problem of false teachers in the first century. These men were described in verses 3-5. In verse 5, Paul mentioned that these false teachers were "imagining that godliness is a means of gain." They thought godliness was a source of profit, a way to make money, or a livelihood. This motivation was completely unacceptable to the Lord. Paul said that godliness, which brings contentment, is a great gain by itself.

In 2 Timothy 4:3, 4 Paul came back to denounce false teachers again. He encouraged Timothy to be different from them, fulfilling the ministry to which he was called. Then Paul explained what was about to happen to himself, for he had eternity in view. "For I am already on the point of being sacrificed; the time of my departure has come. I have fought the good fight, I have finished the race, I have kept the faith. Henceforth there is laid up for me the crown of righteousness, which the Lord, the righteous judge, will award to me on that Day, and not only to me but also to all who have loved his appearing" (1 Timothy 4:6-8).

There are some who feel that the "crown of righteousness" each believer is to receive at Christ's second coming will represent one's worship capacity in heaven throughout eternity. The crown will be a symbol of what the believer has accomplished for Christ here on earth.

The Apostle John gave us a glimpse of how we will use our crowns in heaven. "The twenty-four elders fall down before him who is seated on the throne and worship him who lives for ever and ever; they cast their crowns before the throne, singing, 'worthy art thou, our Lord and God, to receive glory and honor and power, for thou didst create all things, and by thy will they existed and were created' " (Revelation 4:10, 11).

This describes the essence of all we have considered in this chapter. God, through Christ, created people and all things they use and enjoy. However, He did not create these things to serve us as much as He did to serve Himself. Those who are motivated by godliness will consecrate themselves and all they possess to the Lord. Then they will be rewarded with crowns to be used in worshiping Him for all eternity. If we keep this in mind, materialism need not distort our lives here on earth.

7   Laying up Treasures

"Lay up for yourselves treasures in heaven" (*Matthew 6:20*).

How would you like to find three million dollars scattered along the highway? A Purolator Security armored van carrying three million dollars in bills and coins from the Dallas Federal Reserve Bank collided with a pickup truck on Highway 149 near Beckville, Texas. The van overturned, the doors flew open, and sacks of money hit the ground and burst open. The three men in the van escaped injury and jumped out to pick up the money. Charles Cammack, an off-duty policeman happened by, mounted the van with his shotgun, and kept passersby away from the scene.

Most of us have probably had dreams in which we found money just for the taking. Then we woke up and realized it doesn't come that easily. In fact, we may be resigned to the thought that we are unlikely ever to have much as far as earth's treasures are concerned. However, there is an urge in us to lay aside something for ourselves, in order to meet emergencies, buy something we want, or save for retirement.

A reasonable savings program is commendable, but we must not become obsessed by it. We have to learn to hold only lightly to this world's things. Even money earning interest in a savings account can rapidly lose its value if galloping inflation undermines our currency.

Far more important to us is the need for laying up treasures in heaven, where they will be preserved and meet us upon arrival in our eternal home. If this is our savings goal, our heart attitude will be the kind God can bless.

Earthly treasures consumed

As children we were entranced by tales of pirates finding treasure-laden ships to plunder. We have thrilled at people following maps leading to hidden treasure chests. We were told of the California gold rush in 1849 and of men picking up nuggets of great worth along the creeks of that state's gold fields. We have heard of individuals finding their pot of gold at the end of a business rainbow. We have marveled at young singers or athletes springing to fame and fortune almost overnight. We have read of gamblers, including state lottery-ticket buyers, amassing fortunes by the turn of a card or the purchase of a winning number.

Follow-up accounts have informed us that many of the individuals involved in these windfalls have not succeeded in using their treasures wisely. Fortunes have melted away as quickly as they came. Disillusionment about what money can buy has plagued some. Fair-weather friends have vanished along with the money lost. Having become used to a high standard of living, those affected found readjustment to modest means extremely frustrating and painful.

In His Sermon on the Mount, Jesus was thinking of these things when He said, "Do not lay up for yourselves treasures on earth, where moth and rust consume and where thieves break in and steal" (Matthew 6:19). He mentioned the two categories by which treasures in His day were eroded. One was by natural means, such as moths eating holes into precious garments. The word "rust" would not apply to gold or silver, for they do not rust, so it probably referred to anything "eating into" a treasure or otherwise consuming or using it up. The other category was that of robbery perpetrated by men. The loss of money or goods even today falls into these two categories.

In spite of the Master's teaching, even one of His twelve disciples allowed greed to control his life. Judas Iscariot was treasurer for the group, and he was a thief (John 12:6). His greed motivated him to betray Jesus for thirty pieces of silver (Matthew 26:14-16). Remorse over his greed and betrayal caused him to commit suicide (Matthew 27:3-5). Greed led Judas to his own horrible place of punishment forever (Acts 1:25).

We must constantly be on guard against greed in our own lives, or it may consume us, as well. Christians ought to set an example for others to follow regarding this matter. If they will make spiritual things predominant in their lives, and material things secondary, they can demonstrate the true meaning of stewardship of earthly resources.

Heavenly treasures preserved

Jesus made clear that there is only one depository where treasures are really safe. He said, "Lay up for yourselves treasures in heaven, where neither moth nor rust consumes and where thieves do not break in and steal" (Matthew 6:20). Neither natural nor human forces can eat away at the treasures sent on ahead to heaven.

Since people are largely earthbound, it took some imagination for them to understand what Jesus meant about depositing treasures in heaven. There is no transfer of material things from earth to heaven. All the Bible ever talks about is the transferal of believers at the second coming of Christ, at which time they will receive glorified bodies equipped for eternity (1 Corinthians 15:51-53; 1 Thessalonians 4:14-17).

Jesus obviously was talking about the deposit of spiritual treasures in heaven. These are to accumulate throughout a person's life. No doubt they will also continue to accumulate after one's death, for one's influence lingers on. When a believer arrives inside the pearly gates, he will be rewarded for his service to Christ and to his fellowmen.

Some of the things a believer can do on earth, which will cause him to deposit heavenly treasures, are intangible. He can witness to others, sympathize with the sorrowful, pray for those in need, and in other ways show his concern. Some of the things he can do are tangible. He can offer shelter, food, clothing, and medical help to the needy. He can contribute to the building and maintenance of churches and extra-church agencies.

The motive behind all these actions will be important when it comes time for rewards to be given. Love for Christ will be the only acceptable motivation. Works on that basis will be counted as gold, silver, and precious stones. Any other works will be counted as wood, hay, and stubble. When the fire of judgment is applied, only the gold, silver, and precious stones will endure, while the wood, hay, and stubble will be burned (1 Corinthians 3:11-15). When Jesus comes, He "will bring to light the things now hidden in darkness and will disclose the purposes of the heart. Then every man will receive his commendation from God" (1 Corinthians 4:5).

Heart attitude considered

Jesus said, "Where your treasure is, there will your heart be also" (Matthew 6:21). He knew that whatever a person counts precious is going to cause him to pay attention to it. Looking about Him, Jesus could see many people devoted to earthly possessions. He tried to help His followers lift their eyes to something better and more enduring. He pointed the way to heaven and urged them to deposit righteousness and good works to their accounts there. It was a difficult task for HIm to perform, and it has continued to be difficult for those who have carried on His work since He ascended back up to heaven.

Man's acquisitive nature militates against the thing Jesus was teaching. Little children learn through their senses long before they are able to use powers of reasoning. They become attached to material things early in life and are very upset if anyone tampers with those things. By the time they mature enough to learn through reasoning and revelation, a pattern has been set. It is an uphill fight to help them see that mental, emotional, social, and spiritual realities are often much more important than physical or material realities.

Their parents, teachers, and other guides would not be able to convince them of the values of the unseen if it were not for the assistance of the Holy Spirit. As they work from the outside of these developing personalities, the Spirit of God works from the inside. Only when they

48

are ready to be persuaded of a proper ordering of their priorities will youngsters have their outlook on life raised to a new level of understanding.

What is true of children is also true of young people and adults. The older individuals get, the more difficult it is for them to make the transition from self-centered thinking to that which seeks the good of others. Some never make it. They live and die with only their own interests at heart.

Believers identified with Christ would do well to heed Paul's advice, as given in Colossians 3:1-4. He said, "If then you have been raised with Christ, seek these things that are above, where Christ is, seated at the right hand of God. Set your minds on things that are above, not on things that are on earth. For you have died, and your life is hid with Christ in God. When Christ who is our life appears, then you also will appear with him in glory." Paul may have been thinking of Christ's teaching, as found in Matthew 6:19-21, when he wrote this passage. In any case, he knew that a person's heart is devoted to what he treasures, and Paul wanted each believer to think more of heaven than of earth.

8   Trusting the Lord

"My God will supply every need of yours according to his riches in glory in Christ Jesus" (Philippians 4:19).

Many people have a tendency to trust the Lord only when disaster strikes. In the summer of 1975, a four-day rain inundated the fertile Red River Basin in North Dakota and Minnesota with a foot or more of water. Over a million acres of crops were destroyed. Governors of those states asked President Ford to declare the region a disaster area, thus making low-cost federal loans available for rebuilding.

No doubt many people were praying in the midst of that disaster. We should ask ourselves if we have to wait for disaster to occur before we trust the Lord to help us. Actually, we ought to make a daily habit of taking our needs to Him and seeking His help in dealing with them. If we did that in small matters, we would be ready to do it in great matters.

In this chapter we want to grapple with some basic questions relating to trusting the Lord. Is it possible for anxiety and faith to coexist? Should we ever ask God for luxuries, as well as necessities? Are we always to be optimistic, expecting victory, or are we sometimes justified in being pessimistic, expecting defeat?

The issue of trusting God is tied to the issue of being concerned about material things. If we can trust Him to take care of us, then we need not be overly concerned about material needs.

Anxiety or faith?

It is difficult to know who was more anxious about life—pioneers settling new frontiers or modern people settled into established communities boasting all the conveniences now available.

A pioneering family had to face many dangers—rampages of nature, attacks by hostiles, lack of medical facilities, shortage of supplies, and other things. However, there was a self-reliance which fostered independence of thought and action. Knowledge that a family could live off the land and care for 95 percent of its own problems brought a certain measure of peace to its members.

A family in a modern community does not face many of the challenges a pioneering family did, but it has stresses and strains of its own. Economic survival, rising crime rates, pollution, traffic congestion, drug-abuse, and other problems characteristic of our society cause alarm. However, educational opportunities, medical and dental care, and all the blessings of modern science and technology are available. The advantages are so great that very few really would want to go back to the so-called "good old days."

The fact is that people in every age have had to cope with a broad spectrum of anxieties peculiar to their own time and situation. If we had the ability to travel through the centuries past and pick out the one where life was best, it is unlikely any of us could agree on which one it was. God has placed us in this age, and we must cope with the blessings and curses it contains. This should be seen not so much as resignation as opportunity to meet our own particular challenges.

We talk a lot about faith, but do we really know what it is? "Now faith is the assurance [substantiating] of things hoped for, the conviction [certainty] of things not seen" (Hebrews 11:1). Faith is based on assurance that what God promises will surely come to pass. Presumption is based on the assumption that what one wants or thinks is reasonable will come to pass. There is a great difference between faith and presumption, but people often get them confused with each other.

Anxiety views the future with fear, while faith views the future with hope. Anxiety wonders how the mortgage or rent will be paid, while faith knows it will be possible. Anxiety wonders if the child will survive the operation, while faith knows he will. Anxiety wonders if the move halfway across the continent is a mistake, while faith knows it is God's will.

Anyone familiar with modern families knows that financial worries constitute one of the main causes for family arguments. In most cases, this may be due to worry about making ends meet. If every family could trust the Lord to supply its needs, this tension would vanish. Anxiety and faith do not operate in the same individuals at the same time. One excludes the other. If we want to be free from anxiety, we must trust completely in the Lord.

Necessity or luxury?

You will note that our key verse for this chapter promises believers that God will supply all their *needs,* not all their *desires.* God obligates Himself to meet necessities, rather than luxuries.

The Apostle Paul was imprisoned in Rome when he wrote Philippians 4:10-13. If he did have any money back home in Tarsus, it was not available to him in Rome. He could not follow his occupation as a tentmaker to earn a living. He had to depend on the generosity of friends for his daily needs.

Epaphroditus used to serve as his link with the believers in Philippi, but Epaphroditus became deathly ill while in Rome and could not make the long trip back to Macedonia to pick up the gifts of the church to Paul (Philippians 2:25-30). When he was feeling better, Epaphroditus did go to Philippi and bring back to Rome the contributions of the believers to Paul (Philippians 4:18).

In Philippians 4:10-13 Paul said he realized the Philippians wanted to help him, but that they lacked the opportunity to do so during that particular period. He didn't want them to think he had been depressed by poverty at that time. He had learned how to be content with a little or a lot. He said that he had whatever strength was needed for doing what Christ asked him to do.

Whether we realize it or not, and whether we will admit it or not, we have many things which really belong in the luxury category rather than in the necessity category. It is amazing how today's luxury becomes tomorrow's necessity, at least as far as our thinking goes. If you want to dramatize this, make a list of what you own and then cross off all the items you could conceivably get along without, if you made up your mind to do so. What is left will help you realize what the vast majority of people in this world have in their possession, and you will see that God has truly been generous to you.

It is difficult for us to make such distinctions. We want to keep what we have, and we want to acquire more. We say we are doing it for our families, or to keep up appearances, or to keep the economy rolling along, or for some other plausible reason. Seldom do we deliberately make cutbacks, unless they are absolutely necessary. God must look at us and marvel at our ingenuity in convincing ourselves that luxuries are necessities.

Victory or defeat?

Should we always be optimistic about dealing with financial and material matters, or are we justified in being pessimistic about them sometimes? Could it be that God uses circumstances in this area of our lives to prod us ahead or push us back into line? Does the Lord work *through* these things, or does He work *above* them?

Your answers to the preceding questions may be determined by your own philosophy and experience in the field of personal economics. Personally, I prefer a simple, direct, and hopefully practical approach. No doubt a middle-class upbringing combines with scriptural study to form the viewpoints appearing here.

A Christian who is living in victory and trusting God day by day can be optimistic about all matters relating to financial and material problems. Surely, the Lord is not going to abandon him anywhere along the line. David wrote, "I have been young, and now am old; yet I have not seen the righteous forsaken or his children begging bread" (Psalm 37:25). Optimism is based on God's sufficiency, not on the believer's wisdom or strength. A

54

person may have to "tighten his belt" and go through humbling experiences while extricating himself from difficult situations, but that can be to his profit.

A Christian should realize that his sovereign Lord can use any circumstances in his life to keep a child of His on the path marked out for him. That includes financial and material circumstances. Sometimes this serves to move the believer ahead, and sometimes it serves to hold him back. If it helps him walk *with* God, rather than *behind* or *ahead* of Him, he should be thankful for it.

A Christian needs to see that the Lord works in the life of His child on a very personal level. He makes contact with him right where he lives. That includes the nitty-gritty level of earning a living, paying for needed goods and services, balancing the budget, and all other aspects of personal economics. Although God sometimes works *above* earthly circumstances, He is more likely to work *through* them to reveal His grace and power, for He knows that is the kind of treatment we need.

9   Learning to Sacrifice

"Present your bodies as a living sacrifice, holy and acceptable to God" (Romans 12:1).

From June 1974 through May 1975, England experienced an inflation rate of 25 percent, the worst in Europe. Thoroughly alarmed, Prime Minister Harold Wilson announced a plan calling for a ceiling of $13.20 a week on pay raises for all of England's workers. At the same time he said he would try to hold basic price increases to 10 percent over the coming year following that. He said such measures were necessary to save the country from economic ruin. It was obvious that sacrifices would be necessary. What was true of England has also been true of many other nations in the world in these economically troubled times.

After many years of self-indulgence, people in highly developed countries may all have to come to grips with a changing economic situation in the world. As the oil-producing nations get richer, the industrialized nations may become poorer. It may be necessary to give up dreams of increased affluence. It may be necessary to give up hope of maintaining the standard of living they now enjoy. It may be necessary to sacrifice what they have and live on a lower standard.

56

Have we forgotten the art of sacrifice? Have we been pointed so long in the direction of self-indulgence that we find it almost impossible to give up what we have? We need to be willing to let go of the things of this world, if God should demand it of us.

A basic consecration

God has been very merciful to us, for He sent His Son to be the Sacrifice for our sins. We deserved to die and be eternally punished for our transgressions, but Jesus took the penalty which should have fallen on us, and now we by faith can be saved and eternally blessed. It was because of this truth that the Apostle Paul urged believers in Rome to consecrate themselves as "living sacrifices" to God. The old animal sacrifices were no longer necessary after Jesus became the only perfect Sacrifice for sin, but those who benefited from what Jesus did for them were challenged to serve as live sacrifices.

A basic consecration is required of all believers who want to please the Lord. He is more interested in this than He is in anything else they might offer Him in return for what He has done for them. To be fully dedicated to God and His will has always been more important to Him than offering up literal sacrifices.

As the prophet Micah in the Old Testament put it, " 'With what shall I come before the Lord, and bow myself before God on high? Shall I come before him with burnt offerings, with calves a year old? Will the Lord be pleased with thousands of rams, with ten thousands of rivers of oil? Shall I give my first-born for my transgression, the fruit of my body for the sin of my soul?' He has showed you, O man, what is good; and what does the Lord require of you but to do justice, and to love kindness, and to walk humbly with your God?'' (Micah 6:6-8).

That was the best men could hope to do under the law. Now, in this age of grace, believers can do even better, for the Holy Spirit dwells within them to help them live righteous and consecrated lives if they will yield to His leading. Maintaining a right relationship with the Lord is necessary before seeking to maintain a right relationship with men.

Some people tend to get this reversed. They feel that if they are devoted to humanitarianism they will rise to favor with God. Actually, they should seek favor with God first, and then manifest the same concern for His other creatures as He Himself does. Consecration to God should precede consecration to mankind.

An outward look

God is inconceivably rich and self-sufficient. He doesn't need anything we have to offer Him, although He does ask us to devote ourselves and all we have to Him. If there is a practical way for us to demonstrate our consecration to God it is by sharing what we have with others on this planet. We need to develop an outward look.

It doesn't take much imagination to realize that a basic consecration to God turns into a consecration to other people. The Apostle Peter left a prosperous fishing business on the Sea of Galilee to follow Jesus in His ministry on earth. Afterward, Peter and others went fishing on the sea again, but Jesus appeared on the shore and they went in to meet Him. Then it was that Jesus asked Peter three times if he loved Him. Each time Peter

58

replied that he did, and each time Jesus challenged him to feed His sheep (John 21:2-17). Peter's ministry was far from over when Jesus ascended. For years after that he traveled about, evangelizing and instructing others.

Uncounted thousands since the first century have followed the example of the apostles and devoted themselves to witnessing and teaching for Christ. Their vertical relationship with God has motivated them to have a horizontal relationship with men. This has involved considerable sacrifice on their part. They have given up hopes of high-paying jobs. They have often lived on subsistence incomes. They have suffered scorn, persecution, and even martyrdom. Through their efforts, the gospel has gone around the earth, penetrating pockets of heathenism from remote jungles to sophisticated metropolises. Their sacrificial lives have been "holy and acceptable to God" (Romans 12:1).

During the 1960s and early 1970s many young people caught a vision of what they could do to aid needy people around the world. Many programs were set up by government agencies and private charitable organizations to channel these altruistic youths into backward areas at home and abroad. By the mid-seventies, however, the pendulum began to swing the other way. College young people again set financial and material affluence as their goal upon graduation. Some of this attitude rubbed off on young people training for church-related vocations, and vacancies in pastorates, missionary candidacies, and other openings occurred.

We may be thankful, however, that the Bible colleges, Christian liberal arts colleges, and seminaries still are attracting large numbers of young people with goals of Christian service in mind upon graduation. The Christian day school movement is growing rapidly. Adult education programs in churches and schools are making progress. Christian publishers are generally prospering. Christian radio and television stations are increasing. Many signs point to a greater outreach by Christians to their world.

A spiritual service

The latter part of Romans 12:1 in the Amplified Bible refers to presenting our bodies to God as a believer's "reasonable (rational, intelligent) service *and* spiritual worship." In other words, Paul thought of consecration as intelligent action, as opposed to the mindless devotion given to idols by the pagans of his day. Peter referred to believers as those who "offer spiritual sacrifices acceptable to God through Jesus Christ" (1 Peter 2:5).

Paul followed up his thought about sacrificial living being an intelligent spiritual service in Romans 12:2 by urging believers not to be conformed to this world but to be transformed by the renewing of their minds. In that way, they could prove that the will of God is good, acceptable, and perfect. The intellect is stimulated by exposure to the principles of God's Word. It is stimulated by the presence of the Holy Spirit indwelling all believers.

If our bodies and minds are completely devoted to the Lord, He will open up all kinds of spiritual service for us. Sacrifice of time, money, effort, and love will be required. The grip of materialism will have to be broken so believers may be free to pursue spiritual goals.

Jesus Christ stands as the Example to imitate, for He gave up more than anyone else could ever give up that He might come to earth. "Have this mind among

60

yourselves, which you have in Christ Jesus, who, though he was in the form of God, did not count equality with God a thing to be grasped, but emptied himself, taking the form of a servant, being born in the likeness of men. And being found in human form he humbled himself and became obedient unto death, even death on a cross" (Philippians 2:5-8).

We ought not to give up something simply in hopes of getting back a greater reward, but the Bible does teach that this happens. By sacrificing ourselves and all we possess for the service of God, we may look forward to enjoying the riches of our inheritance in heaven for all eternity. Paul wrote, "I consider that the sufferings of this present time are not worth comparing with the glory that is to be revealed to us" (Romans 8:18).

Believers who learn to sacrifice please God, help others, and improve themselves. They grow in sympathy and love toward others. They become humble. They produce fruit which will bear eternal rewards. They receive more than they give away. Our age needs such believers. Let the fulfillment of that need begin with us.

10   Planning a Budget

"Which of you, desiring to build a tower, does not first sit down and count the cost?" (Luke 14:28).

It was the beginning of the summer, and O. C. Helton pitched a tent for his four daughters and moved a trailer onto his 10-acre lot near Darrington, Washington, for his wife, his son, and himself. The 6-foot-8-inch logger began to build a log cabin to house his family. It was an art learned from his father and grandfather as a youth back in North Carolina. Then Snowhomish County Building Department officials took him to court for failure to get permits for the trailer and cabin.

Officials claimed Helton's building plan was illegible, but he said he lacked the $500-$1000 it would cost to have an architect design it. The jury deliberated an hour and found him innocent of both charges. The big man broke down in tears, remarking, "Now I can finish my cabin before the bad weather sets in." With little education, he planned a home for his family for only $3,400.

We need more individuals with ingenuity such as that in our world today. While doing their appointed tasks, we might hope that government officials will make allowance for this kind of creative approach to the problem of living expenses.

62

Wherever we live, we have to fight a daily battle against costs. One of the most sensible ways to do this is to set up a budget and then live within it. This chapter seeks to provide some guidelines for doing that. General suggestions will be made, and you will have to work out the specifics yourself.

Considering routine needs

Rich people may find it different, but middle- and lower-class people normally have to pay out most of what they earn for routine living expenses. These cover a wide range of items, which may sometimes defy categorization, but we will attempt to list some.

Housing is a basic routine expense, and it can eat deeply into a family's income. There are either mortgage or rental charges to pay, plus bills for improvements, gas, electricity, water, telephone, and perhaps even sewer and trash collection services. One rule of thumb some follow is that housing costs ought not to exceed 30 percent of the family income.

Family expenses include a wide variety of things— allowances, appliance repairs, clothing, dry cleaning, haircuts or styling, hardware, magazines, newspapers, supermarket items, and toys for children. We might also add such things as automobile or other transportation costs, books, Christmas gifts and supplies, other types of gifts, photo supplies, postage expenses, vacation expenses, and normal medical and dental care.

Taxes on the local, state or provincial, and federal levels are constantly rising. In some countries they take up to 40 to 50 percent of a family's income. Sales taxes, property taxes, personal income taxes, school taxes, and many hidden taxes take a large bite out of every budget.

Contributions to churches and charities, along with various extra-church agencies, might also be classified as routine expenses. The reason for this is that Christians are expected to give regularly to the Lord's work and to programs of a humanitarian nature. These four categories—housing, family expenses, taxes, and contributions—account for most of our spending. The only way to cut back in these areas is to thoroughly analyze each type of expenditure and see if it can either be eliminated or modified in some way. Comments on deciding what are necessities and what are luxuries, as provided in Chapter 8, might be considered in this regard. There is a great psychological advantage to making cutbacks on a voluntary basis, rather than being forced to make them against your will. Most people wait until they are forced to cut back, and then they tend to be bitter about it.

Money-management experts might be consulted to see if they have suggestions which could lessen routine expenses. Sometimes it is better to rent than to buy a house, to lease an automobile than to purchase one, or to file individual tax returns than joint ones. Those who work with money all the time are up on these things and can share their expertise with others at a reasonable fee, which can easily be paid with the money saved.

We live in an age of accountability in financial matters, and just keeping a family operating is an extensive business. It is wise to keep a daily record of all income and expenditures, no matter how small. The daily record can be transferred over to a monthly record, and finally an annual summary can be produced. This makes it possible to come up with correct figures for tax computations, applications for loans or credit purchases, and assessments on how to plan for the future.

Our handling of resources ought to be more than merely receiving income and parceling it out with the help of coupon books. If we are going to have any control over our money, we will have to work out a comprehensive budget and then try to stay within it. This will also help us plan to make funds available for whatever special and emergency needs we may have.

Considering special needs

Aside from, and in addition to, the routine needs we have, there are special needs which come along and have to be paid. These will vary with ages of family members and circumstances affecting them. Let's think of some hypothetical examples of what this means.

When children come into a family, special furniture and supplies have to be acquired for taking care of them. A family might go out and spend a small fortune on this, or it might get secondhand things, use shower gifts, or borrow items from relatives and friends to help cut costs. If any of the children is handicapped, special equipment might be required. Sometimes government agencies or charitable organizations have funds available for this.

Children who have respiratory problems may need tonsillectomies, and some of the cost will not be covered by the family's hospitalization plan. Older children may need to have their teeth straightened. Teenagers may need special sports equipment or musical instruments. Adults may decide the house needs to be remodeled or enlarged to allow for family growth.

Caring for such needs might be postponed or taken care of in stages, but eventually they demand that something be done. Credit is rather easily obtainable today, and families find it normal to get loaded down with so many bank loans and expense accounts that it is extremely difficult to get out from under them. Some may file for bankruptcy.

Common sense dictates that families ought to anticipate special needs as they come along, making plans to pay for them. If this can be done out of savings, much interest otherwise paid out for credit can be saved. If that is not possible, borrowing at a bank is usually cheaper than paying the high rates of charge accounts. It is probably best not to borrow from relatives or friends, although there are exceptions.

Considering emergency needs

Hopefully, emergencies do not arise often, but there are times when they demand outlays of money not in a family's routine—or special-need categories. These are usually connected with some disastrous development. A member of the family can have an accident and be severely injured, requiring surgery and a long convalescence. Another member may be stricken with a serious disease or develop an abnormality such as a defective heart valve. Here again, extensive medical treatment will be required.

The family house may burn down to the ground. The main wage earner may lose his job, become chronically ill, or die. An unavoidable accident with the family car may lead to a lawsuit, resulting in the award of a large amount of money in damages to the complainant. A long list of possibilities could be compiled, any one of which might plunge the family into a financial crisis. We think of such things as happening to other people, but they *could* happen to us.

Our first reaction is to become obsessed by panic, but that will not help anything, and it could make the situation worse. We need to remind ourselves "that in everything God works for good with those who love him, who are called according to his purpose" (Romans 8:28). If the Lord allows a crisis to come into our lives, He must have some reason for it. James said such a trial serves to make a believer develop strength of character. If the believer wants to know God's reason for allowing the trial, he need only ask Him and He will reveal it, but this must be done in unwavering faith (James 1:2-6).

We have reserved consideration of insurance expenses until this time. Although these are routine, in the sense that they are paid along with other routine expenses, they are designed to cover emergencies. Some Christians may frown on insurance policies, thinking they demonstrate a lack of faith in God's care, but others accept them as a means of good stewardship.

In cases where savings, insurance coverage, or other resources for meeting emergencies are lacking, the community of believers ought to generously donate help to those in need. This is a practical way to show Christian love and concern.

11   Uniting with Others

"So then, as we have opportunity, let us do good to all men, and especially to those who are of the household of faith" (Galatians 6:10).

Mrs. Rosalie Oldham was driving a pickup truck carrying twenty-five beehives northwest of Phoenix, Arizona, when her brakes failed. As she tried to pull off the road, the truck overturned, and thousands of bees surrounded the truck, stinging her over 100 times. State troopers tried to rescue her, but they were driven back by the cloud of bees. A helicopter brought in experts from a honey company in Phoenix. Protected by special suits, they put down a smoke cloud which drove the bees back to their hives. Mrs. Oldham was taken to a hospital in Wickenburg, where she was reported in satisfactory condition.

Here was a case where a person had to have help from others, or she could have died. One of the most terrifying things that has happened in our modern world is the frequent lack of compassion for individuals in trouble. Fortunately, these are isolated incidents. Most people will still lend a helping hand when disasters of one kind or another strike.

Within the Christian church there should be a spirit of

love and concern which operates all the time. It is by uniting with other believers within the family of God that we can face the future courageously. This can have significance for our material concerns and for our contributions toward the needs of others.

Victims of manipulation

The Latin slogan, "*caveat emptor,*" means, "Let the purchaser beware." In other words, whoever buys something does so at his own risk. There are no guarantees for the product. There are no warranties to cover repair costs if something goes wrong. The philosophy behind the slogan is that an unwary customer deserves to be hoodwinked. But such an attitude falls outside our system of Christian ethics.

We live in a world where slick businessmen take advantage of the fact that some customers are indeed stupid or careless. If these businessmen can manipulate a customer into buying some service or product which does not measure up to acceptable standards, they may feel they have enhanced their reputation for shrewdness. It is individuals such as these who make life difficult, not only for customers, but also for honest businessmen of high principles. Better Business Bureaus do what they can to warn the public, but these unscrupulous men still thrive on gouging the unsuspecting.

Do Christians have any means by which to escape this kind of manipulation? Do they have any advantage over unsaved people who have to deal with the business world? The first thought which comes to mind is that believers can pray about their purchases, asking the Lord to show them what to buy and what to avoid buying. If God is concerned about all aspects of our lives, then He is concerned about helping us avoid evil men in the business world.

Another thing Christians can do is to spread the word among other believers whenever they find businessmen who are honest and dependable, whether those businessmen are Christians or not. It often pays to go out of one's way to find such persons and do business with them. By patronizing them, they are assured they will not have to stoop to unscrupulous practices to stay in business. They should be rewarded for operating above-board.

A third thing Christians can do is to put individual and collective pressure on businessmen who are victimizing people. They must be very careful how they do this. Street protests, boycotts, and other such tactics are undignified for Christians to use, and they must always remember that even unscrupulous businessmen are potential believers. Nothing should be done to alienate them and cut off a witness to them. What Christians *can* do, however, is to quietly discuss with them why they should change their ways and how good business practices build up a steady clientele in the end.

Cooperative business ventures

In Chapter 4 we considered the communal life of believers in the early church in Jerusalem. We mentioned various utopian schemes which were tried as experiments over the years. Although some might disagree, the prevailing conclusion has been that communal living has generally been short-lived. It has been put to general use only in totalitarian nations, such as Red China, where the people have been forced into communes if they resisted. A study of the Bible would show

70

that there is nothing inherently wrong in private ownership, unless the person involved makes it more important to himself than God or anyone else.

What can be done to merge the best aspects of communal activity and private ownership? In some places the answer appears to be cooperative business ventures. Farmers have made good use of this, setting up farm-supply businesses in which individuals hold shares. They are able to buy products and services at reduced prices, or they receive rebates at the end of the year after paying standard prices. Since their volume of buying is large, they are entitled to wholesale prices. Local individuals are elected to boards which run the enterprises in their area.

It may be that Christians in a particular area could establish something similar to this to benefit from good products, honest service, and reduced prices. Shares could be sold, Christian leaders elected to boards, and Christian employees hired to operate the enterprizes involved. This is not socialism, but rather cooperative Christian effort in business ventures. Private ownership on the individual level need not be jeopardized. Membership in the cooperative would be completely voluntary, and anyone who wanted to get out could do so upon proper notice.

It is best if churches themselves do not try to set up cooperative business ventures. Some have tried it and regretted the results. Churches seem to serve their communities best if they limit themselves to spiritual and educational ministries. This need not rule out church-operated schools, bookstores, radio or television stations, and other enterprises dedicated to spiritual and educational objectives. Organizations such as Goodwill

Industries and the Salvation Army operate business ventures to help the poor and the handicapped, and this seems to be most commendable.

Sharing one's resources

Uniting with other believers to solve material and financial problems will often produce charitable sharing of one's resources with another. The Bible has many passages which encourage this. Solomon put giving on a high level when he said, "He who is kind to the poor lends to the Lord, and he will repay him for his deed" (Proverbs 19:17). Solomon also said, "Cast your bread upon the waters, for you will find it after many days" (Ecclesiastes 11:1). Paul reminded believers of "the words of the Lord Jesus, how he said, 'It is more blessed to give than to receive' " (Acts 20:35). Time and again, Paul urged Gentile believers to make donations for the poor saints in Jerusalem (2 Corinthians 8—9). The key verse for this chapter showed him urging the Galatian believers to "do good to all men, and especially to those who are of the household of faith" (Galatians 6:10). The writer of Hebrews said, "Let brotherly love continue. Do not neglect to show hospitality to strangers" (Hebrews 13:1, 2). Many other references on this subject could be quoted.

A disturbing development in modern times is the lack of concern many Christians have for others who have needs. Perhaps this is due to several factors. People tend to gravitate toward churches containing those of their own social class. Thus, people in churches which have middle class and upper class members and attendants may see no need for sharing material resources with others in their own congregation. The government has

72

such extensive welfare programs that some Christians shift the burden for the needy to government agencies or to private charitable organizations. Sometimes racial prejudices keep them from seeking out the needy and offering them help.

Something more should be done by church people than putting a dollar into the "deacon fund" or "benevolent fund" each month or quarter when communion is served. If a man in the congregation is out of work, church people should be alerted and do whatever they can to help him find a job. If a disaster hits a family, everyone should contribute whatever money, time, labor, or other help is needed. Prayers should ascend for all those experiencing financial difficulties. Christianity is not so lofty that it cannot show concern for problems at the personal level. An individual or family should feel a sense of security, not only in God, but through being wrapped up in the fellowship of the church congregation. It is tragic and unfortunate that this sense of well-being is missing in many church groups.

Giving is not so much an obligation as it is a grace. Paul wrote, "Now as you excel in everything—in faith, in utterance, in knowledge, in all earnestness, and in your love for us—see that you excel in this gracious work also. . . . For you know the grace of our Lord Jesus Christ, that though he was rich, yet for your sake he became poor, so that by his poverty you might become rich" (2 Corinthians 8:7, 9).

12   Rediscovering People

"If we walk in the light, as he is in the light, we have fellowship with one another" (1 John 1:7).

Some people were resistant to the influx of Vietnamese refugees into the United States after South Vietnam collapsed, while others found in this a wonderful opportunity to rediscover the joy connected with helping others.

Assemblyman Rolland E. Kidder of Jamestown, New York, found it necessary to be absent from the state capital at Albany to help a family of Vietnamese refugees. He received a telegram from the Red Cross, informing him that Van Trung Thu and his family were at Indiantown Gap in Pennsylvania. Kidder had known this man while serving in the Mekong Delta, so he wanted to resettle him and his family in Jamestown.

On a day when no session was scheduled, he made plans to drive down to Pennsylvania and take the family to Jamestown. Then a session was unexpectedly called. The problem was solved when Governor Carey arranged for a state plane to fly to Pennsylvania and transport Kidder and the Vietnamese to Jamestown. Kidder was back in Albany by noon and attended the scheduled session. Then he drove to Jamestown, found the family a house, the man a job, and arranged for a church to act as the Vietnamese family's sponsor.

This kind of thing, in less dramatic fashion, was going on all over the country, as 130,000 refugees were absorbed by compassionate people. It was a timely lesson, for people are more important than things, and we need to rediscover that fact.

Rediscovering family members

Missionaries have told us that they fall in love with the people they serve in foreign lands. When asked what is different about those people, they often say they are more genuine, sincere, unhurried, sympathetic, and concerned about one another. The missionaries prefer them to many of their own countrymen. Have we lost something vitally important in our fast-paced, materialistic way of life? It would seem that we have.

That doesn't mean we cannot recapture the love for people which we have foolishly transferred to things. Our rediscovery will have to begin at home with members of our own families. That may be much harder than we think it will be. We may not realize how easily and quickly family members drift apart.

It usually begins in the teenage years, when sons and daughters become involved in after-school activities. Practice sessions for athletics, musical activities, club programs, and even church-sponsored activities may run up through the supper hour, so the contact made by family members is destroyed. Part-time jobs can do the same thing. Some teenagers get summer jobs away from home and are gone for weeks or months.

Adult family members also may get so busy with evening and weekend activities that they are gone most of the time other members are home. Trips away from home may be necessary to pursue certain kinds of vocations. It gets to the point where home appears to be only a stopping-off place to grab a bite to eat or snatch a few hours of rest at night.

We have to realize that "togetherness" can be over-emphasized. It is natural for children, young people, and adults to want to be with those of their own age and interests. Parents cannot really be the kind of pals their children need or want in the way those their own age can, and the opposite is also true. However, the typical modern family could do more to provide opportunities for its members to do some things together. Each family will have to work out the details for itself. The parents will have to take the initiative for this in most cases, but teenagers might surprise them and do it, too.

Knowing the members of one's own family in a loving and close relationship can make up for the loss of many material things. It is regrettable that this fact is often learned only after it is too late, with the children grown up and gone. Nothing material we could give one another is more important than the gift of ourselves to one another.

Rediscovering Christian fellowship

Have you ever noticed how some people enter and exit from church on Sunday or any other day? They hurry in just before programs, sit through them, and hurry out just as fast. They never attend a church fellowship supper, Sunday school picnic, or any other activity designed to help them get acquainted with other church members or attenders. They never let their names go up for positions on committees or for church offices. They almost treat church contacts as if they were necessary evils for remaining in good standing, but things which must be kept to a minimum.

The Lord surely did not mean for members of the body of Christ to be that alienated from each other. Jesus "appointed twelve, to be with him, and to be sent out to preach and have authority to cast out demons" (Mark 3:14, 15). If the Son of God felt a need for companionship in His ministry, we certainly should feel that need, too.

It is difficult for individuals who have shunned fellowship with other believers to change their patterns. God will have to break in upon their complacency and stimulate them to make such a change. They may feel ashamed that they have neglected fellowship with other believers, and this can be a powerful deterrent to making the contacts they know they should make. Sometimes disaster has to strike before they will seek the fellowship to be found in the company of other Christians. It is the responsibility of others in the church to overlook their former aloofness, welcome them warmly, and involve them in their fellowship activities as soon as possible.

Christian fellowship ought not to be limited only to those of one's own particular church. In most communities there are other true believers who attend elsewhere, but they will be happy for contacts beyond denominational lines. A wide variety of mutual interests and activities can be shared with them. Some cooperative efforts can accomplish what no one church could do by itself. Extra-church agencies have probably done more to break down the barriers between Christians than any other groups have.

Once we get acquainted more with other believers, we

will rediscover their value to us personally. When life becomes difficult, it is much more comforting to have a Christian friend bow in prayer with us than it is to try to find comfort in an expensive house, an ornate automobile, or a cold bank account. The greatest thing about heaven will not be its pearly gates or its streets of gold. It will be fellowship with God and Christ, as well as with the redeemed of all ages. We can prepare for that now.

Rediscovering prospective believers

Outside the circle of the family, and outside the circle of Christian friends, there is a community of lost people who need the gospel of Jesus Christ. Paul said, "Conduct yourselves wisely toward outsiders, making the most of the time. Let your speech always be gracious, seasoned with salt, so that you may know how you ought to answer every one" (Colossians 4:5, 6). He was telling believers to be gracious in their contacts with the unconverted. He was telling them to be characterized by the "fruit of the Spirit" (Galatians 5:22, 23), so they could truly be "the salt of the earth" and "the light of the world" (Matthew 5:13, 14).

It is easy to develop a holier-than-thou attitude and to look condescendingly on the unregenerated. Some Christians deliberately limit their contacts with the unsaved, fearful they might spiritually contaminate themselves otherwise. Some look on sinners with nothing but disgust and seek to separate themselves from them as much as possible. They have only the short view. They fail to see what those sinners can become, if the grace of God is applied to their lives.

There is wisdom in refraining from intimate association with those who are not born again, but to cut off

78

normal channels of communication with them is to cut off opportunities for witnessing to them. They need to see examples of righteous living displayed before them from day to day. It is difficult to put up with their lying, foul-speaking, cheating, selfishness, and sinful habits, but Christ died for them. Believers are charged with the responsibility and are blessed with the privilege of persuading sinners to find salvation through faith in Jesus Christ.

One of life's greatest blessings is to win souls to Christ, to see converts develop spiritually, and to enjoy their friendship during the years ahead. A bond is established between those who witness and those who respond which can be precious and enduring. It is possible that the best friends you may ever have are even now in the grip of Satan, but by your efforts they will come into the family of God.

Money and all the things money can buy will never provide the satisfaction which friendship with other human beings can supply. It is time we awoke to that basic fact of life and began to cultivate our relationships with others, whether they are within our own family circle, the larger circle of Christian acquaintances, or the even larger circle of potential believers.

13   Recognizing Free Values

"Now we have received not the spirit of the world, but the Spirit which is from God, that we might understand the gifts bestowed on us by God" (1 Corinthians 2:12).

The paintings of two French families, believed to be the Khans and Schreibers, went on the auction block at Sotheby's in London. Fifty impressionist paintings were involved, including five Pissarros, five Monets, four Bonnards, a Matisse, and a Picasso. Within seventy-two minutes $5.5 million worth had been sold to an eager group of 500 bidders. The largest sale was $462,000 for Monet's "Cathedral at Rouen," which went to a Swiss art dealer.

It is difficult for those of us who have modest incomes to know how it feels to have wealth in the hundreds of thousands of dollars or in the millions. We may be somewhat envious of them, but we comfort ourselves by remembering that many rich people have been unhappy, finding their wealth lifts some burdens from them but adds others in their place.

The purpose of this chapter is not to encourage enjoyment of things which are free, simply because of a "sour grapes" attitude toward things which cost money. What is intended here is an attempt to make us recognize, as the popular ballad stated, that "the best things in life are free." If we can be convinced of that, then we can order our priorities properly and keep materialism secondary in our thinking.

Nature's free gifts

When God created this earth, He furnished it with all that people would need for their sustenance and enjoyment, as far as material things go. "And God saw everything that he had made, and behold, it was very good" (Genesis 1:31). We would expect nothing less than perfection from a perfect God. Because man sinned, a curse was imposed on the earth, and some of that perfection was lost (Genesis 3:17, 18). However, the earth still is blessed with untold resources for the good of mankind.

Although there are wide variations in climates, the earth orbits about the sun at just the right distance to keep it from either burning up or freezing into a lifeless ball. Those holding an evolutionary theory regarding the origin of life claim this fact explains how life developed on the earth, but those who believe the Bible's creation account say that God positioned the earth precisely where it is to sustain life here.

As humans, we are tied to this earth. The only ones of us temporarily to escape from it have been the astronauts, and they had to carry an artificial atmosphere with them while out in space. Through science and technology, we have succeeded in drawing from the land, the water, and the air all the marvelous things we use and enjoy. More has been done along this line in the twentieth century than in all the preceding centuries combined. We do live in an unusual and wonderful age, even though we chafe at some of its problems.

Enjoyment of nature's gifts depends a great deal on a person's attitude and circumstances. One man will look at a jungle, mountain, river, lake, or desert and think of it only in terms of an obstacle. Another will look at the same thing and see in it many things to appreciate and enjoy. One's background and the ability to cope with a particular natural environment make the difference in such cases.

There is a great movement back to the land in our day. People are moving out of urban areas, not only to suburbia, but to exurbia and to rural and wooded areas. Vacation homes are being constructed in many isolated locations. Existing lakes are rimmed with cottages, and new lakes are being created for further settlement. Hiking trails, bicycle trails, and recreation areas are providing opportunities for people to get close to nature again. As new highways probe back into previously impenetrable areas, more and more people will be able to take advantage of this trend.

Mankind's free gifts

We could think much about all the monuments to human ingenuity which have been built here, but that would be only one aspect of this subject. It is true that our culture has produced many fine things to enjoy, and has made many of them available to others without charge. Scholarships provide educational opportunities for the poor and handicapped. Government grants help people overcome by disasters. Charitable organizations spend billions every year on programs to assist needy people. If we took the time, we could think of many examples of free things available to all.

However, our desire here is to consider the more important resource of people themselves. One cannot buy real friendship. It has to be freely given, and when it is given it is a valuable gift to enjoy. We need to develop meaningful relationships with people, not because of what they *have* in the way of material things, but because of who they *are.* If we could strip away all their material status symbols and know them in a one-to-one manner, we might find them quite different from what we thought they were. They might find us quite different, as well.

Now comes an important question—Who are you? Are you really a nice person to know and to be with on an extended basis? If you had to leave everything you own behind and start life in a new setting, would you be the kind of individual others would love?

Since the matter of rediscovering the importance of people was dealt with at some length in Chapter 12, we are not going to spend much time with it here. We just need to remind ourselves often that, next to God, people are our most valuable resource. They ought never to be placed in an inferior position to material things in our thinking, or we will lose our perspective.

God's free gifts

There is no better way we could close out this book on overcoming materialism than to emphasize the gifts God has freely given to us. A complete list would be so long that it could not be included. All we can do is to think of some of the main ones and praise Him for them. "In him we live and move and have our being" (Acts 17:28). In other words, all we have comes from Him.

James said, "Every good endowment and every

perfect gift is from above, coming down from the Father of lights" (James 1:17). Whatever evils we have to contend with obviously came from Satan below, but let's consider the good things and not the bad.

The most obvious gift we have is that of life itself. If our health is good, then the gift of life is to be greatly appreciated. If our health is poor, at least we can be thankful for what physical strength and abilities we do have. We can trust God for grace to endure afflictions and hope for deliverance in due time. Individuals ought never to complain about being born. Their mothers went down to death's door to welcome them into the world. The Lord permitted them to be here, and that is a gift which should be appreciated, even when things become difficult.

The material things God has given us, or which He has helped us to acquire, should be accepted as gifts from His hand. Except for His sustaining power, we could have none of them. The thrust of this whole book has been to keep our evaluation of material things in line with the use God has for them in our lives. We do not despise material things and become ascetics, but we do not let them master us, either.

The intelligence we have comes from the Lord. It may not be as great as we would like to have, but it is worth more to us than material things. If we were idiots living in the midst of luxury, chances are we would be miserable. It is better to be intelligent and be poor than to be the other way around. Enjoyment on a sensual level may appear to be the keenest kind a person could have, but some have discovered that enjoyment on a mental level can be even better.

The gift of family and friends should rate high on our

scale of appreciation for what God gives us. Without them, life would lose its meaning. One of the worst punishments a person can have is to be placed in solitary confinement, shut up unto himself for days, weeks, months, or years on end. It has driven some people insane.

The most important of all gifts, of course, is eternal life. It provides hope in this world, and it points us ahead to the world to come. The only way an individual can have eternal life is to put his faith in Jesus Christ and the atonement He made for sinners at Calvary. Once that individual is identified with Christ, he can look forward to inheriting all that heaven has to offer.

"Blessed be the God and Father of our Lord Jesus Christ! By his great mercy we have been born anew to a living hope through the resurrection of Jesus Christ from the dead, and to an inheritance which is imperishable, undefiled, and unfading, kept in heaven for you, who by God's power are guarded through faith for a salvation ready to be revealed in the last time" (1 Peter 1:3-5).

Gordon G. Talbot was born on June 17, 1928, in Utica, New York. He earned a BA at Houghton College, Houghton, New York (1949); a ThB at Nyack College, Nyack, New York (1951); an MA at Wheaton College, Wheaton, Illinois (1956); and a PhD at The School of Education at New York University in New York City (1968). He pastored churches in New York State and Nebraska and served as a director of Christian education in a church in Des Moines, Iowa.

Most of Talbot's career has been devoted to teaching—at Bryan College, Dayton, Tennessee; Houghton College, Houghton, New York; Detroit Bible College, Detroit, Michigan; Canadian Bible College/Canadian Theological College, Regina, Saskatchewan; Winnipeg Bible College/Winnipeg Theological Seminary, Otterburne, Manitoba; and Christian Schools, Inc., Glen Cove, Maine, of which he is currently president.

Talbot has been writing curriculum materials since 1963 for various evangelical publishers, and spent 1971-1975 full time in this ministry.

Talbot was "founder" of the National Association of Directors of Christian Education, in the sense that he served as chairman of the Steering Committee of that organization from 1960 to 1961 and as its first president from 1961 to 1962. He is a member of the National Association of Professors of Christian Education. Along the way, he has found time to publish some two hundred articles on Christian education for such periodicals as *Moody Monthly, The Sunday School Times* & *Gospel Herald,* and *The Good News Broadcaster.*

He married Janet Tuttle of Manchester, New York, on August 20, 1949. The Talbots have a son, David, born in 1958, and an adopted daughter, Carol, a Korean orphan born in Seoul in 1959.